AUTHENTIC COLD CALLING: The Path to Fearless, Effective Cold Calling

A Fast, Proven, Effectual

Cold Calling Roadmap

designed to move you beyond

the fear of cold calling to

financial success by being authentic!

"Anyone, in any type of sales, can only benefit if they'll only apply this simple method in all their business dealings."

By Gregory Priola

enlightenedcoldcalling@gmail.com

Copyright © by CCSG Group LLC

Copyright, Legal Notice and Disclaimer:

*All rights are reserved.
No part of this publication may be reproduced, stored in a retrieval system or transmitted in any form or by any means, electronic, mechanical, photocopying, recording or otherwise, without prior permission of CCSG Group LLC.*

Please note that much of this publication is based on personal experience and anecdotal evidence. Although the author has made every reasonable attempt to achieve complete accuracy of the content in this book, he assumes no responsibility for errors or omissions. Also, you should use this information as you see fit, and at your own risk. Your particular situation may not be exactly suited to the examples illustrated here; in fact, it's likely that they won't be the same, and you should adjust your use of this information these recommendations accordingly.

Cover design by Kristi Came
http://www.kristicame.com/

Special thanks to George S. Wilson for his invaluable input.

This book is dedicated to my good friend and business associate Dave who made me realize that it's not the people that stand by your side when you're at your best, but the ones who stand beside you when you're at your worst that are your true friends.

TABLE OF CONTENTS

PREFACE

WHO THIS BOOK IS FOR

INTRODUCTION

CHAPTER ONE: COLD CALLING - LOVE IT OR HATE IT

    You Hate Cold Calling

    You Love Cold Calling

CHAPTER TWO - BUILD A QUALITY PROSPECT LIST

    Cold Calling Databases

    Formatting Cold Calling List Excel Sheet

    Cutting and Pasting Final Cold Calling List

    Identifying Warm Leads

    More On Identifying Decision Makers

CHAPTER THREE - MENTAL, EMOTIONAL, PHYSICAL AND SPIRITUAL PREPARATION

    Mental Preparation

    Emotional Preparation

    Physical Preparation

    Spiritual Preparation

CHAPTER FOUR - THE ART OF COLD CALLING PROSPECTS

    Scrap The Cold Calling Script

Times and Days to Call

Set Your Intention Before Calling

Don't Argue, Don't Defend, Always Play Nice

Call Your Warm Leads First

Contacting Decision Makers

Turn Gatekeepers Into Allies

It's All How You Say It

The Warm Lead Pitch

The New Business Pitch

The Win-Back Pitch

Don't Stop Once You Start

Use Your Intuition

CONCLUSION

PREFACE

"Everyone thinks of changing the world, but no one thinks of changing himself." - Leo *Tolstoy*

It would have been ideal if a book like this were available when I first started my sales career. If I had been aware that an effective, practical, unscripted and authentic method of cold calling was available I would have made a lot more money and experienced much less anguish. Of course the Internet didn't exist and Steve Jobs was still inventing the future in his garage; however, the basics and the sheer simplicity of this cold calling system are as applicable today as they were then.

Through experience I learned that the way I was taught to cold call was laborious, painful, often humiliating and for the most part unproductive. I read all the latest books on sales tactics and pitches, attended numerous sales seminars and training classes yet found nothing that would improve my cold calling experience. I could sell but I did not have an effective way to get in front of the prospect in order to close the deal. It was only when I threw out every cold calling book, script or reference to the standard way of doing things and devised a better path.

After years of calling thousands of prospects I believe I have a process that is not based on being a numbers game, actually it's just the opposite. It feels comfortable, is incredibly effective and avoids a scripted, intrusive manner of cold calling that accomplishes my intention of setting an appointment in a matter of minutes.

This is not a lengthy book, full of fluff, statistical data, psychological theories of prospects reactions, etc., nor does it tell you exactly what you must say and do. It is based on my twenty plus years of cold calling prospects and asking for their business or at a minimum, agreeing to meet with me. I have learned how to avoid the deflation that rejection can trigger and I know how to easily and effortlessly adapt my pitch to whatever reactions I encounter.

If you read this book and follow my simple suggestions you too will find that cold calling can be easy and financially rewarding. I will show you how to find entirely FREE prospect databases, how to build and create a qualified prospect list, ways to discern a warm lead from a cold lead, and dependable sources you can use to identify the decision maker.

Also you will discover the importance of mental, emotional, physical and spiritual preparation before you ever pick up the phone. I will guide you through the actual cold calling process beginning with days and times to call, how to deal with gatekeepers, assistants and receptionists, and explain a free flowing style of cold calling that is adaptable to your personality and *will* generate new business for you.

I state in this book a few times that I do not hold all the answers, and indeed you may not agree with all my pointers. And suggestions for improvement are always welcome by me. I urge you to think for yourself and to discover the "authentic self" that is within you because that is the key to your ultimate success: not only with cold calling but in your sales career and life in general for. "To thine own self be true, and it must follow, as the night the day, thou canst not then be false to any man."

As I said previously, if you are searching for long, drawn out theories, scientific data to reinforce every concept I present or psychological evaluations of how prospects think, STOP here and begin the refund process! I have been tremendously successful at cold calling by being short on conversation, clear on intent, purpose and value, and by being my authentic self. My intent is to present you with the basic tools necessary for developing your own style of enlightened cold calling. I guarantee if you change yourself from a fearful, insecure, self-doubting "salesperson" to a caring, open, honest and concerned solution provider your sales numbers and bank account will soon validate the power of this positive transformation.

WHO THIS BOOK IS FOR

I primarily wrote this book for B2B telecommunication sales reps but in actuality it applies to anyone that would call a complete stranger with the intention of meeting them or convincing them to take some sort of action. If you are cold calling on a weekly basis for new business this book will be of tremendous value to you. If you desire to call just one person or maybe a few individuals to accomplishment a goal this book will assist you in carrying out that mission. Here are a few examples of those who can benefit:

1. All telecommunications sales reps
2. Sales reps seeking new business
3. Non-Profit fund raising campaigners
4. Those seeking employment
5. Writers/Talent looking for agents
6. Be creative and list some more beneficiaries

INTRODUCTION

"Some day people will learn that material things do not bring happiness, and are of little use in making people creative and powerful." - Charles Proteus Steinmetz, Inventor Of The Alternating Current Motor

If you are reading this book chances are you were referred to it by your employer, a trusted friend, an associate, or you found it on the internet. It really doesn't matter how you arrived, the fact is you are not here by accident, so I want to tell you what you can expect from this book.

First and foremost if you believe this book will turn you into an overnight cold calling sensation and that your revenue will increase tenfold over the next month you are either completely delusional (don't worry at times I excel at this disorder) or deeply mired in the low-performing habits of highly successful mediocre sales people.

I won't make such unrealistic claims simply to motivate you to read this book. I hope you are here to discover a way to make effective unscripted cold calls without experiencing nausea, cold sweats, extreme terror or any of the other numerous maladies I have witnessed, and experienced myself, over the years. I truly want you to succeed at cold calling. Overcoming the dread and fear of cold calling will propel your sales efforts forward at a quickened pace.

I have read many of the books and courses available that tout "cold calling scripts that work" and cold calling principles that are effective, methodical, scientifically and psychologically based. Quite frankly, are a load of crap. It is my opinion they are outdated, archaic, manipulative, slights of hand that will only bury you deeper into the depths of cold calling despair. So take a breath as I assure you I will spare you from similar rhetoric.

If you are reading this book because you know that cold calling is still a viable and essential aspect of generating new business then I can offer you a practical roadmap, for lack of a better term, to guide you past the absolute fear and apprehension you may encounter when faced with having to make a cold call. You will also realize that personal effort and a high degree of inner motivation are required to become successful at any sales technique.

I have written this specifically for the B2B telecommunication Business Account Consultant/Representative/Executive (or insert your title here) that are in the field and actually pay a visit to existing customers and qualified prospects. I do believe the contents and instructions contained within this volume can be slightly modified and still prove applicable for inside sales reps as well. Actually the system and principles outlined in this book can and will work for anyone in any type of sales field that wants to excel in their chosen profession.

Also be aware that I write this as if we were at the local coffee shop and I am sitting directly across the table from you sipping my double espresso loaded with extra whipped cream. It's conversational, informal, and at times you may note my rather dry and not vaguely sardonic attempt at humor. The reason for my casual writing nature is quite simple. I am not a professional writer! I'm just a fellow that has literally called thousands of strangers and asked them for either their business, time or money or any combination of the three and have had astounding results.

So let me tell you how this all came about as I was not born to be a mystical telemarketer or a sage to the telecommunication pros.

In another lifetime I was a producer of theatrical plays in Los Angeles. I was a producer for *Bleacher Bums*, "The longest running comedy hit in LA" with Joe Montegna, *Zen Boogie The Musical*, *Hippodrome*, to name a few, as well as producing concerts for major musical acts of that era. As a *Producer* I was expected to *produce* results and get things done. I had a purpose and had zero fear when it came to calling anyone for anything. I left the entertainment business when I realized I didn't want to be married with children in that environment. I moved back to the Midwest and decided upon a career that I thought would offer the same emotional buzz and egotistical stimulation as show biz did. So I convinced a successful financial firm into sponsoring me and I became a Series 7 Stockbroker.

Wow, what a cluster that turned into. When I first started I sat in a bullpen, yep, just like the movie *Wall Street* starring Michael Douglas and Charlie Sheen, depicted. I was given a quota of 250 cold calls per day. Think about this! 250 cold calls a day to business owners, executives, known investors, retirees and so on, without any lists other than outdated ones supplied by the brokerage firm and a current telephone book. I pitched a $20k position in highly rated, fully insured, AAA mutual bonds that were currently yielding the best possible return at the time and I called twelve hours a day just to meet my quota. Occasionally, much to my utter amazement, someone would say YES. I'll never forget that first YES I heard because after I picked myself up off the floor in sheer astonishment, I had to put the customer on hold for the longest time as I had to solicit help to complete the order. I didn't have a clue!

For the first time in my life I experienced the queasiness, anxiety, fear and "time travel" thought process (more on this later) that occurs when faced with the fact that I had to pick up the telephone and ask a complete stranger for his money, trust and time; all of which I did not consider myself to be worthy of. Oh, the despicable things I have done in my life! And on and on ad nauseam.

Unfortunately for many, yet propitiously for me, on a crisp Monday morning in mid October of that year stock markets around the world plummeted. The Dow dropped 508 points to a low of 1738 and as abruptly as the market failed so did my financial services career. But all was not lost.

I returned to my radio, TV and telecommunications roots and took a job as the marketing director for one of only five companies in the United States that was producing all the multimedia aspects necessary for the implementation of a POS kiosk. Attention all geeks, at that time there was no such beast as digital formatting and a 1 gigabyte external hard drive was the size of a shoe box. The good news was I knew how to call decision makers at Fortune 500 companies and I knew what to say to them based on what I learned from my cold calling days at the brokerage firm. Computers and lists with names and numbers were at my fingertips and I rapidly excelled.

Now fast forward to my entry into the world of telecommunications. I became immediately adept at utilizing sales tools provided by the national telecommunications provider for whom I was an authorized distributor. I knew how to develop abundant and likely successful lists and I did just that. I worked with a small group of sales pros that knew the ins and outs of the telecom business and we all loved what we were doing. It soon became apparent that we could become even more effective and financially successful if I stayed in the office and cold called existing customers and new biz prospects with the sole intention of getting the prospect to agree to a face to face meeting with one of my sales associates. I was setting appointments for four sales reps and by necessity developed a precise and concise pitch that worked more often than not.

The reason I'm telling you all this is because I want you know that what I'm sharing with you was not something I just nonchalantly threw together with the hope of making a few bucks. Generating a few dollars is cool don't get me wrong, but what I am sharing with you is based upon a natural devolution from fearless and motivated Hollywood producer to stark raving mad man with high anxiety cold call methods; and then my evolution to confident and adept motivator of prospects who utilized a basic system day after day, week after week, month after month because it worked. I also do not make a hundred calls to get one appointment. It now takes me as few as five and at most twenty five calls to get at least two appointments.

Remember, I can only tell you how I do what I do. Nothing I write about is etched in stone as everyone has their own unique and perfect personality. I expect you to question some of my processes and methodology as I believe we all can add to any mouse trap and make it better. Consider this as your basic GPS that can help you navigate past the fear, anxiety ,and repugnance of cold calling.

I love the Geico commercial where Pinocchio is featured as a quite unsuccessful motivational speaker. He begins his seminar by stating, as he looks around the room, that all he sees is unlimited potential. Immediately his nose begins to grow. Pinocchio points at a front row attendee and states, "You have unlimited potential" as his nose extends to even greater lengths, and he repeats this mantra till his nose is three foot long at which time, in his high pitched and child like voice a despondent Pinocchio murmurs, "Oh no." It's hilarious and I promise I won't be Pinocchio and fill you with BS.

One word for any of you tech savvy pundits that think cold calling is a dinosaur and only employed by the unsophisticated and computer illiterate...REALLY...REALLY! Consider this quote by Steve Richard, co-founder and head of sales training at B2B consulting firm Vorsight, who was hired by a Fortune 500 wireless telecom company to train their reps the art of cold calling. Here it is as posted by the *Harvard Business Review*, "As social media and web applications have become the hottest networking tools in business, too many sales managers are burying the cold call as an obsolete business practice. If you fall in this category I've got news for you: the cold call is not only alive, it's kicking. And it should be utilized by every B2B sales force."

As you read this book please keep in mind that I do not believe in hard sales tactics, prospect manipulation, or pushy and desperate measures as they are ineffective and I personally find them ethically and professionally dishonest. I want you to begin to see yourself as a trusted expert in your field, an advisor, provider, and mediator, an individual genuinely concerned who wants to provide a solution that is appropriate to customer's needs. You are not in this business just for the money. You strive to make an honest connection with every prospect you encounter by creating a bond based on trust. You do not pursue a potential client if you realize that your product and/or service is not a good fit. You stop selling to meet a quota. These will become the hallmarks of your successful cold calling experience. I write this book with only you, the reader, in mind; and my prayer for you is unlimited success in all you choose to attempt and accomplish in life.

I write this book with only you, the reader, in mind and my prayer for you is unlimited success in all you choose to attempt and accomplish in life.

CHAPTER ONE: COLD CALLING - LOVE IT OR HATE IT

"There are two basic motivating forces: fear and love..." John Lennon

Believe this or not but there are some individuals in existence, in every avenue of sales, that love cold calling. I happen to be one of these rare folk. OK, love can be an overused and ambiguous term with many implications so for the purpose of this book and our discussion let's define "love" as having something you can count on, are genuinely comfortable with and won't hurt you or make you cry your eyes out.

You Hate Cold Calling

I used to hate cold calling until I started hating not having new customers more. But let's face reality here, we are rejected in some way, shape or form on a daily basis so what sane and emotionally balanced individual would knowingly invite rejection into their life? You are selling telecommunications so we can immediately reject the sane and emotionally balanced excuse and cut to the chase. You suck at cold calling: ergo all the anti-cold calling "experts" are justifiably correct and it's a waste of time. Right?

Other common excuses brought into play when debasing cold calling are, "I don't want to sound desperate," "I don't want to impose on people," and, "I really don't know what to say or do." to name a few. The last excuse is the more accurate as, by no fault of your own I might add, you have been figuratively thrown into the gladiator arena without any weapons to protect yourself from impending doom.

Most of us have been told we must cold call to generate new business, armed only with some very basic cold calling sales training that is mainstream garbage and ineffective at best. Or we were sent forth to cold call with no training at all as we were hired with the assumption that we were great at what we do and only product knowledge is necessary. I am not implying that this is the circumstance at your company, just that being set up for failure does occur from time to time.

I don't want to dwell on this negative topic much longer and I only have a couple more issues to address. How many of you can honestly say you believe in the products and services you are selling? This is vital to your success in the telecommunications industry or in any sales venue for that matter.

When I was a stock broker I would drive analysts crazy because I could see through their thinly veiled attempt to convince me that a certain stock or bond issue was a good investment. I knew and even understood the technical, quantitative and analytical analysis involved when evaluating and rating a stock or bond. I also knew that brokerage firms offer too many stocks and bonds as a sound investment based on the amount of money the firm has vested in the underwriting of the issue. Many times I would refuse to even present the product to my clients because I didn't believe in it.

If you are presently experiencing this type of doubt about the products and services you are selling I strongly urge you to pack up your desk right now and save yourself and your employer a great deal of future grief. No amount of training will surmount the negatives you believe to be true about the products you are representing on a conscious and subconscious level.

Last but not least is a lack of belief in yourself and your sales abilities. This does not apply to you veterans unless you are in a serious slump. To the newbie don't be hard on yourself as the myth that some were born sales people is simply that, a myth. Most of the time poor performance can be attributed to a lack of focus, lack of a consistent system, and poor time management, all of which can change once the problems are identified, addressed and corrected.

Pinpoint the top producers on your team and mimic what they do. You will soon discover they are successful because they have a system that works, they repeat this process day after day, and they rarely deviate from what works for them. I have always found top producers are glad to share their knowledge with newcomers who initiate the contact and have proven they are seriously motivated to move to the top. Vilfredo Pareto's principle states that, for many events, roughly 80% of the effects come from 20% of the causes or as it applies to sales, 80% of a company's sales are made by 20% of its sales staff. Strive to be part of that 20% and know that effective cold calling is one way to achieve that goal.

You Love Cold Calling

Here are the top three reasons I love cold calling:
1. I KNOW I will increase my revenue.
2. I KNOW I will keep my job.
3. I KNOW management will stay off my ass because I am a producer.

I have other reasons that I'll share momentarily but take a long hard look at my top three reasons why I love cold calling. Who doesn't want to make more money? Name one sales person you know that entered the sales profession just to get by. We all gravitated to sales because of the profession's powerful allure that big bucks could be made sometimes quickly and that we have a certain degree of control over our time and future.

Effective cold calling so dramatically improved my bottom line that I couldn't help romancing this reciprocating object of my attention because it sated by basic lust for money. I find pockets full of cash very sexy! Call me shallow but be honest, you find it sexy also.

As a sales producer, the fear of failure and the brutal possibility that I would be fired for lack of performance never entered my realm of possibilities. Oh, I have lost jobs and been fired before but never for lack of turning numbers and not meeting quota. I have always lived life my way and on my terms and yes I can hear you musing, "Hmmm, how is that working out for you?" Sometimes up, sometimes down, but it's all good and for a purpose.

I have learned to hit the delete key when it comes to the need to understand everything that happens in the journey of life. How does this relate to cold calling. It doesn't but if you're someone that requires the safety and comfort that job security presumably offers to feel warm and fuzzy then indulge me if I veer off course as my intention is to enable you to experience success as you define it.

Ever been called on the carpet by your boss for not meeting quota? Dictionary.com explains the origin of this term; " This term began as **on the carpet ,** which in the early 1700s referred to a cloth (carpet) covering a conference table and therefore came to mean "under consideration or discussion." In 19th-century America, however, *carpet* meant "floor covering," and the expression, first recorded in 1902, alluded to being called before or reprimanded by a person rich or powerful enough to have a carpet."

Your sales manager may or may not be rich and powerful but I assure you they have a carpet and you only want to stand on it while receiving an "atta boy or girl." Cold calling kept my numbers high and I always managed to fly under the radar so to speak.

Another reason I love to cold call is the fact that cold calling allows me to create opportunities for myself on a daily basis. In all my years of selling I can't recall one time that a customer, without a referral, called me asking me for my business. Not once! I choose to be successful and I accomplish that objective by being grateful for what I do have, relying on myself to be motivated and by putting one foot in front of the other every day.

I always believed that I could personally help a prospective customer by providing a viable and cost effective solution for their needs. Then and now, I cold call a prospect with the awareness that what I offer them is a solid, valuable, and operative remedy or alternative that will only enhance their current communications position.

I don't cold call with a self-serving, manipulative, just want a deal attitude. My intention is to get the appointment so I can help them gather all the information necessary in order for them to feel comfortable with their buying decision. I only want what is best for the customer and have walked away more than once because what they had wasn't broken and didn't need fixing.

Cold calling is not a numbers game as most claim it to be. At least it isn't for me and it doesn't have to be for you. You can only take so many rejections before the ego shuts you down. I spend a small amount of dedicated time cold calling with wonderful results and you can also if you following the simple recommendations I am about to deliver.

CHAPTER TWO - BUILD A QUALITY PROSPECT LIST

"I love lists. Always have. When I was 14, I wrote down every dirty word I knew on file cards and placed them in alphabetical order." Adam Savage - Co-Host MythBusters

OK, you Google "quotes for list making" and top me if possible. That aside, I cannot express the importance of completing this first step. If you don't take the time and put in the effort to create a quality, customized prospect list all will be for naught. Fortunately for anyone in the telecommunications industry, every business is in need of the services and products you provide.

NOTE - Don't compile your calling list while you're at the office. You are burning valuable selling time as it takes a few hours of concentrated time to build your list. Do your list construction at home during the evening or put aside a few hours on the weekend to accumulate your cold calling list.

I understand many of you have pressing responsibilities outside the office, children, spouses, spouses who act like children, elderly parents, stress relieving hobbies, etc. I am not saying this is a weekly chore or a long-term project; however, it will serve you well as a qualified list for three months or more. So if you only have to do this exercise a four times a year and it will boost your income and sales status, it's time well spent.

Cold Calling Databases

There are a multitude of companies on the internet offering their sales lead databases for an annual or per list fee. I am completely in opposition to giving away my money to such companies. Number one reason is the cost. At one time I did opt for a paid service and ended up signing a contract for $1200 a year. While I recouped that initial investment several times over, I discovered I was able to obtain the same information for free at the library. Most public libraries in the United States have at least one major sales lead database provider you can access at home, online, if you have a local library card. I know this for a fact as I checked out public libraries online in several major markets and did not find one without a free database available for library cardholders. These free databases are usually found on the page of the Business Resource tab, which you can find on your libraries home page. If you have trouble finding the databases just call the library. They are always willing to assist.

My public library offers AtoZ Databases and I use AtoZ free of charge as often as I need to. The only difference between free (library) databases and paid databases is the number of businesses you can download per search. If you have a paid database you can select and download substantially more business selections during one search session; while most library databases allow a maximum of 1,000 downloads per visit. This can be surmounted as follows: Be careful to select your downloads from the types of companies you will be calling upon. (e.g. If you are not going to be calling on national chains, don't select those types of businesses to download.) Concentrate only on the types of businesses that fit your profile, and download the maximum number allowed per visit. If you wish to download more, simply sign out, sign back in and resume downloading. While this tends to be tedious, I promise you; it's worth the effort!

Many of you are assigned territories such as certain zip codes and/or small market cities so stick to your fixed parameters when designating search criteria. Databases have "Search By" considerations that you can choose when developing your list such as Geography > City, State, Zip, Keyword, Business Size > Employee Size and Annual Revenue. For most lists I create I select City, State, Zip, Business Size > Employee Size and Annual Revenue. City, State, Zip are obvious choices and I like the Employee Size and Annual Revenue because I can sort my list by the annual revenue so I have an idea of how large the prospective account could be. Call it elephant hunting if you will. A blend of elephants and rabbits (smaller accounts) constitute a great customer blend and the rabbits close much quicker.

The best method is to try this yourself, play around with it, and, after some experimentation, you will engender lists suited to your needs.

Formatting Cold Calling List Excel Sheet

I am assuming that the reader is familiar with Microsoft Excel. If you are not, you can find helpful tips in the tutorial of the program. There are also several instructional books which are simple and user friendly.

Once you have made your company selections from the database download the list in the default format which is either an Excel or Excel(CVS) file. If you have a choice in the matter always select the basic Excel option.

When you open the downloaded file you will see approximately eighteen (18) columns with a heading for each column. For our purpose we are only concerned with copying and pasting nine (9) of these columns. But first you will have to create a new sheet to copy and paste these nine (9) columns onto.

At the bottom of the sheet it will say ""First Sheet" in the tab and if you place your curser on the small sheet icon just to the right of the "First Sheet" tab "Insert Worksheet" becomes visible. Click on "Insert Worksheet" and a new sheet will appear titled "Sheet Two." Rename the new worksheet by right clicking on "Sheet Two" and rename it "Zip XXXXX" or "City Name," or anything that reminds you of what it contains and the word "Final." So an example would be "Zip 46804 Final" or "Fort Myers Final" and this is also the name you want to save the file as in your "Lists Folder."

On the renamed sheet click on "Page Layout" tab at the top of the page then select "Margins" > "Custom Margins" and set the "Top:" at 0.25" the "Bottom:" at 0.25" then "Left:" at 0.2" and "Right:" at 0.2" then save settings. Next click on "Orientation" and select "Landscape." Now find "Gridlines" which is located just to the right from where you have been working and check the "Print" option and then save your work.

Now you are ready to copy and paste all necessary data from the original downloaded data sheet to the "Final" sheet you just created to complete your cold calling list.

Cutting and Pasting Final Cold Calling List

As I noted previously we are only interested in cutting and pasting nine (9) of the available columns from the original downloaded data sheet. The nine (9) columns are, and *in this order*, **Phone, Business Name, Physical Address, City, Zip, Executive Name, Title, Revenue/Yr, Notes**. After coping and pasting the nine (9) columns onto your newly created "Final" sheet, the sheet should now look like this: NOTE: Due to page printing constraints I am not able to expand each column to fit the pasted data. You can extend each column's width to allow all pasted data to show in each column. **Due to Kindle formatting requirements I had to put the nine columns in sections. On your sheet, the nine (9) headings will appear as a complete row.**

PHONE	BUSINESS NAME	PHYSICAL ADDRESS
555-555-1212	XYZ CORP	1 MAIN ST.

CITY	ZIP	EXECUTIVE NAME
YOUR CITY	55555	ALFRED E. NEWMAN

TITLE	REVENUE/YR	NOTES
THE MAN	300,000,000	APPT. SET

Now perform a "Print Preview" then close the preview and the page breaks for each sheet will be visible and two (2) or three (3) blank columns should appear to the right of your basic nine (9) columns on the sheet. Expand the **NOTES** column's width to the end of the page break and your sheet is ready for entering notes and almost ready for printing.

Before you print the final prospect list highlight only the columns you are going to print and when the "Print Dialog Box" pops up check "Selection" in the "Page Range" area. If you do not highlight and check "Selection" you will print off 100 or more blank sheets so please don't overlook this step.

In the next chapter we will discuss the importance of identifying all the "warm leads" on your list. As you move through the warm leads discovery process you can type notes on your existing sheet as you go along or print the prospect list first and write your notes in by hand. I personally print my list first then enter all notes by hand with a red pin. Writing my notes by hand works for me but as I said before, we are all divinely unique creatures so whatever way you do it is cool.

Identifying Warm Leads

Most of you know the difference between a warm lead and a cold lead but for those who don't I'll briefly state the difference. In our business a warm lead is an existing customer that presently utilizes at least one of your products or services. A cold lead is a prospect you want to convert to your products and services and one you have never contacted nor have they initiated any contact with you.

Warm leads are a fantastic opportunity for you as warm leads are more willing to meet with you and more likely to advance to the next level of services or products if their needs mandate a change. It's likely your sales manager provides warm lead lists for your team or has access to such lists so just ask them if one exists or can be generated.

As for your recently created list you want to start identifying your leads as warm or cold. This can be a bit time consuming but armed with a multitude of warm leads your cold calling venture will be much more pleasant and prosperous.

Start by either printing your list or have it open and accessible on your computer. You have customer relationship management (CRM) systems such as Salesforce at your fingertips that are instrumental when attempting to identify warm leads. Enter the prospect info into your CRM system and if it hits as an existing customer you simply add into the notes section of your list what products and services they have along with the contact name and phone number.

I always used a red pen and hand wrote this information on my list because the red notes stood out and are easy to read plus I didn't like going from the CRM screen to my open list on my laptop. It's simply a matter of choice so do whatever works for you.

Write or type in what products and services they have in short code such as int. for internet, vid for video and V for voice or your own devised code that makes sense to you. Another step I take to help identify the decision maker is to Google the company and if they have a website I go to the "Contact Us" page or the "About Us" page and there I usually find the decision maker. Add this information into the notes section also.

As I stated earlier none of my suggestions are set in stone so tinker, tweak and customize my process to fit your habits and patterns. Always room for better mouse traps and most of you are younger, better looking and brighter than I so knock yourself out.

More On Identifying Decision Makers

Identifying your warm leads should prove to be an easy task when utilizing your CRM system. Finding the decision maker for your cold leads can be more of a challenge but is not impossible. The free databases and even the paid for databases will not always have the name of the decision maker. We need to discover the decision maker within any organization and I have had success at discerning who they are using several methods.

First let's list some obvious decision makers; for a small business it's usually the owner, for middle size companies start with the CFO for this is ultimately a financial decision, for larger companies again the CFO is a good place to start or call for the IT department manager. In non-profit organizations always start with the Executive Director and follow the lead from there.

I love top down selling, which is a contact referral from upper management or the owner. If the owner, Executive Director or CFO refers you to someone else then you have been given a golden egg. Now when you call the contact that upper management has provided for you, all that is necessary is for you to set the appointment day and time. For example: "Hi Mark, my name is (your name) and I'm with (your company). I just spoke with (name the CFO, owner or upper management contact) and he/she asked me to give you a call to set an appointment with you so I can supply a quote for our services." Almost never fails. What are they going to say? I really can't recall a referral given to me from management telling me they weren't interested. What employee is going to question management's decisions?

If the generated list does not provide a contact name there are some quick solutions available that will help with identifying the decision maker. First Google the company and check out the "About Us" page, the "Contact Us" page and also look for a "Our Staff" page. Between these three pages you are likely to find the decision maker or at the least a viable contact to start with.

I also try Manta.com, Linkedin, and Facebook. Write down every name you think may be the decision maker as you have to start somewhere. Most of the time you will be able to identify the decision maker from one of these sources.

So your cold calling prospect list has been created and all warm leads identified with product and contact info entered. But before you take a deep breath, pick up the phone and start dialing for dollars, let's explore some preliminary action points you need to be aware of before the first cold call is ever made.

CHAPTER THREE - MENTAL, EMOTIONAL, PHYSICAL AND SPIRITUAL PREPARATION

"Before anything else, preparation is the key to success." Alexander Graham Bell

About now you may be asking yourself, what is this dude talking about? Mental, emotional, physical and *spiritual* preparation before cold calling! Do cold calling cults exist and am I being recruited and initiated into one?

I'm not asking you to drink the spiked kool-aid and lay down just yet, only to consider a short routine that I find helpful before indulging in any cold calling foray. I find my standard practice relaxing, centering, rejuvenating and it sets me in a frame of mind to succeed. I am firmly convinced that success is accomplished first on an inner level. Once I establish the internal feeling and emotion of achievement I move forward enthusiastically, usually with rapid positive results.

Athletes, top executives, entertainers, in fact all high achievers in all walks of life know what I'm saying is true. Henry Ford said, " Whether you think you can or you think you can't, you're right" and long before Henry, Buddha piped, "The mind is everything. What you think you become."

I have found that if I don't prepare myself before I start cold calling it soon becomes laborious, frustrating and a huge waste of time. My preparation doesn't require a significant amount of time and reaps generous benefits. The following are some simple ideas that help put me in the right inner frame of mind to succeed.

Mental Preparation

Your mind desperately wants you to know it is THE MAN, it is THE BOSS! The mind or the ego if you will, is continuously telling you to go, go, go, do more of this, control this situation, you have to be right, be perfect, and anything else necessary to keep you very busy and unaware.

This relentless motion allows the ego to do what is does best: worry, fear, obsess, regret, project, capitulate, think, thINK, THINK until.......

you crash and burn!

So it's time to tame the wild beast before it tames you and completely takes over all control. You do this by first refusing to play along. When the BS starts I immediately step back and try to objectively listen to what my ego is saying. Like a silent observer standing in the shadows, out of sight, yet aware. I don't judge or condemn my thoughts I only let them flow avowing not to get sucked into the negativity, emotion and turmoil of them. Resisting is counterproductive because the more we resist the more the turmoil tends to persist.

Eckhart Toole said it best, "Not all thinking and all emotion are of the ego. They turn into ego only when you identify with them and they take you over completely, that is to say, when they become "I". So I go to the moment of NOW which really pisses the ego off because without a past or future to dwell on the ego has no control and loses its power.

Switch your thoughts to the moment of NOW and begin to understand that at this very moment you are whole, complete, worthwhile and successful. Stop the time traveling which is visiting the over and done with past or vaulting into the non-existent and unpredictable future.

Set your intention to enthusiastically be present NOW in your cold calling effort. State that you will confidently proceed and make a decision to use your mind. Don't let it use you! This works for others and me have confirmed it works for them as well.

Emotional Preparation

Emotions are not good or bad - they just are. They can make us aware of real and impending danger but can also trigger hardwired responses from past situations. For instance your boss calls you in and states: "Your sales are down and you haven't hit quota the past two months." Panic sets in, negative and fearful emotions escalate and a scenario is played out: Boss PO'd > I don't have a job > no job no money>no money no food no home>I have to live in the woods>real tribal head hunters do exists>my tiny head ends up on bosses key chain. While this picture is extreme, it is an example of how our emotions can lead us into a dire expectation of the future.

So my point here is to do your best to avoid any negative situations or negative and emotionally trying people prior to your cold calling. After you have blocked out some time to cold call steer clear of anyone that literally sucks the energy from you. You know who they are in both inside and outside office. They come in all shapes and sizes and they know how to push your buttons, so the best remedy is to avoid them when possible. Remember, you can't change people, and sometimes you can't change that they are in your life, but you can change how you react to them. The idea is to get yourself feeling good before you cold call. Emotional balance and just feeling internally well will definitely increase your prospect calling success rate. Some of my tactics include calling to mind that I have much to be grateful for, thinking about those I love, and tapping into a sense of contentment.

There is nothing better than being honestly grateful for everything you have. Start with the obvious such as your home, car, job, spouse or significant other, children, money, and then for the simple things you possess. Be grateful you have vision to read this book, you had ready access to food today, you have indoor plumbing and safe water to drink. There are literally millions of people in this world that do not have even the basic necessities of life. So cheer up mate, if your reading this you're not one of them.

I actually tingle inside when I think of how much love I have for my children. I don't let the trials and tribulations of raising them even enter my thoughts. I experience only the raw emotional charge of love that I feel from the core of my being. You may not have children but odds are you have someone you care about this deeply so just get lost in that love for a bit.

On a metaphysical note I firmly believe that everything that has happened has a purpose and that what will happen is for a reason and that at this very moment, this very moment of NOW, all is well and just as it's supposed to be. Learn to hit the delete key when it comes to understanding why. Accept that it is what it is and accept where you find yourself today. Fighting against what is or complaining about circumstances won't change a thing. So refuse to "do pain" as my friend Stuart Wilde puts it and love your completely imperfect, perfect self as best you can.

Physical Preparation

We all know that we should treat our bodies with love and care for optimum physical performance. What you eat, the hours you sleep and the exercise you get are basic elements that will dictate your level of daily energy and well-being. I am not going to delve into a full regiment that you could adhere to on a daily basis. Taking care of yourself physically is a personal choice so I am confining this discussion to physical preparation the day before you cold call and the day of cold calling.

Sleep is good! A good night's rest does more than reduce embarrassing puffy eyes. As studies show sleep also plays a critical role in the function of the immune system, metabolism, memory, learning, and other vital functions. I can tell the difference on a physical, mental and emotional level if I only get six hours of sleep as opposed to eight hours of sleep. Get eight hours of sleep the night before if at all possible.

Avoid drinking alcohol the night before cold calling as alcohol disrupts the sleep cycle and, if you imbibe too much, a hangover is hardly the best way to prepare for your cold calling process. Don't eat junk food the night before or the day of calling, as junk food is low on nutrients and high in sugar and will deplete your energy quickly. If you are cold calling in the afternoon steer clear of a heavy lunch so you won't feel like crawling under your desk for a nap instead of dialing for dollars.

Coffee is actually healthy in moderation and I love a cup of freshly ground dark roasted coffee in the morning. Coffee can boost your energy, improve memory and mood but without temperance coffee can cause jitters, restlessness, nervousness and a host of other harmful symptoms. So don't whack out on Starbucks before you start your cold calling session. A cup in the morning and maybe a cup before you begin your prospecting is cool and shouldn't negatively interfere with your performance.

I'm a walker not a runner. I started playing rugby when I was seventeen years old and ran daily, sometimes up to ten miles a day. A rugby match consists of two 40 minute halves, with no time outs I might add, a 10 minute half time break and played in all weather conditions. I had to be in top shape to play the game. Little did I know that all the running I did would have adverse affects on my body in later years. So now I walk as much and as often as possible and especially like walking in the rain.

Walking is a gentle, low impact, free and easy form of exercise that has numerous positive health benefits. A short brisk walk is one of the best natural energizers around. If you possibly can, take a quick stroll around the building or up and down flights of steps before you begin calling. If you can't walk do some stretching exercises, yoga movements, jump to conclusions, push your luck, or any other physical activity that will get the blood flowing before your cold calling session.

Spiritual Preparation

I don't discuss sex, politics or religion so don't get up in arms over this section's title. It is not based on any sect, denomination or organized religious beliefs. What I want to touch on is how to surrender to the moment and to be completely aligned with your intentions.

I do subscribe to the philosophy that we are all spiritual beings having a human experience. The human experience explains our tendency to "time travel" which is obsessing over past disappointments and subjecting ourselves to anxiety over perceived future events that don't exist. The past and future are just reminiscences and speculations over which you have no control. You don't have to live in this bondage because you can always choose to live in this very moment.

If your intention is to be successful in cold calling and sales in general, learn to surrender thoughts of the past and worries about the future on a moment by moment basis if that is what it takes for you. Tame the wild pony before it runs wild and stomps you into the ground.

No one is immune to the human experience. We all have financial, familial, personal relationship, and self worth concerns but when they start to surface try to temper them with the confidence that you have done all you can in preparation for the best possible outcome. We have no actual control over what will be so the best course of action is to surrender the results and proceed with a positive and expectant attitude.

I would never consider cold calling prospects if I'm mentally and emotionally in a dark, negative, and fearful place. None of us are immune to down days or even weeks for that matter. It's all part of life and the trick is recognizing where you are, acknowledging it and waiting it out. Remember, what you resist persists. I can't say this enough. I have learned it the hard way and you don't have to repeat my mistake.

After preparing mentally, emotionally and physically before I attempt anything the odds of falling into spiritual despair are slim to none. These practices are actually tools to be used when you intend on enjoying life right now, in this very moment, and are determined to be completely present in all your choices and decisions.

If you have followed my previous suggestions you know how to build a quality prospect list, how to prepare yourself mentally, emotionally, physically and spiritually. Now all you need is the proper technique, which we shall cover in the next (and final) chapter. This chapter will cover the actual cold calling process including when to call, how to make your presentation and handle any unexpected situations which may arise with the various people you encounter.

CHAPTER FOUR - THE ART OF COLD CALLING PROSPECTS

"Ask and you shall receive. You must, yourself, do the asking...Mediocrity is self-inflicted. Genius is self-bestowed." Walter Russell

You realize cold calling is a vital aspect of the selling process and effective cold calling bypasses the indiscriminate "numbers game" mentality. Cold calling is an art form that combines product knowledge, clarity of purpose, professional communication abilities, and a sensible solution for your prospects needs.

All great business leaders, entrepreneurs, and top sales producers know and posses these abilities or they wouldn't be where they are today. They are willing to fail in order to succeed, know they make their own "luck," push themselves out of their comfort zone, ask for what they want, and set focused, realistic goals that are obtainable. Additional traits also exist, so use your imagination, name a few more and dwell on the traits you now posses and the ones you intend to develop.

Now it's time to create your own success. You have created a quality prospect list, identified the warm leads complete with contact info, prepared yourself mentally, emotionally, physically and spiritually so let's put all the pieces of the puzzle together as we delve into the actual methodology of cold calling.

Scrap The Cold Calling Script

Good people of Earth, if you have a cold calling script in your possession I want you to throw it in the trash can right now! There is no such creature as the "winning script" or the "cold calling script that works," as touted on countless websites or by your colleagues. Scripts are a waste of time, ineffective and actually an insult to the prospect. So shred and burn any canned piece of rubbish that you may have collected from any source and erase the pitch from your consciousness.

How many times have you received a cold call yourself and the caller begins with, "Hi Mary, how are you today?" Boom baby....out of the gate you know what the call is and you are immediately annoyed because this person wants to know how you are. Small talk is awkward when you have no idea who the person is and in your heart you know this poor schmuck doesn't give a rats ass how you are.

"Is this a good time for you?" is usually the next scripted question. Hmmm...let me think about this, "OH HELL NO!!!" One person out of 100 will tell you now is a good time to chat and it's because they are drunk, high on dope, a combination of both, or they just got fired and want to screw the company on the way out, or they are closing their business for good and want to sell you their assets. I can't comprehend why some companies or sales reps still subscribe to such an archaic and abominable practice. I could rant more about scripts but I think you understand my general disagreement with them.

Instead of utilizing unnatural and coined scripts I want you to learn to rely on your authentic self for effective dialogue when cold calling prospects. Using your natural cadence, sincerity, and confidence, you can begin your cold call with a non-linear approach that allows for the prospects unscripted reaction to anything you say. Scripts are linear tools and when interrupted creates a tailspin the salesperson has difficulty recovering from, if they do at all.

I cold call with the intention of setting an appointment so I get to the point of my call quickly, avoid any small talk and offer a valid and beneficial reason for meeting with me. I am flexible as to what I say but usually stick to a basic pitch that feels natural, relaxed and comfortable. I try to match the tone, rhythm and timbre of the individual I am speaking to as studies have proven mimicking enhances the success rate of sales. I don't consider this to be misleading or manipulative as I have personally discovered it actually puts the prospect at ease on a subconscious level and more willing to honestly open up to me.

My basic pitch also creates an opening for the prospect to engage in a two way conversation and piques their interest as I always present a financial savings and/or a solution to a telecommunications problem. I will be sharing a few of my pitches with you but before I do I want to cover a few more cold calling preliminaries.

Times and Days to Call

By trial and error I have found certain times of the day to be more advantageous than others for cold calling prospects. As a matter of fact, Dr. James Oldroyd from the Kellogg School of Management, recently compiled data from a million cold calls and confirmed what I believe to be the best days and times to cold call prospects.

Never cold call on a Monday unless you have been given a referral and you are confident they will be receptive to you. You know what your Monday is usually like and the same circumstances apply for your prospects.

Thursday should be your first choice as the week is winding down and prospects are more relaxed and willing to talk with you. I rank Tuesday and Wednesday second and third, respectively. Friday morning has yielded fair results for me but Friday afternoon is not very productive as the decision maker is gone already or has their mind on more relaxing matters other than business.

The best time of day to cold call if you want reach the decision maker is between 8 - 9 a.m. followed closely by the 4 -5 p.m. slot. I have had great success calling between 11 a.m. - 12 noon, and from 2 - 3 p.m., of course never calling during the lunch hour. If you encounter a "gatekeeper" (more about them later) that is impossible to pass call before 8 a.m. or after 5 p.m. as they will not be in or gone for the day and the targeted contact usually answers the phone. Let's recap:

BEST TIME OF DAY TO CALL	BEST DAYS TO CALL
8 a.m. - 9 a.m.	Thursday
4 p.m. - 5 p.m.	Tuesday
11 a.m. - 12 noon	Wednesday
2 p.m. - 3 p.m.	Friday mornings
Before 8 a.m. or after 5 p.m. if gatekeeper	Never call on a Monday

Cold calling does not have to be a long drawn out ordeal. Just devote a couple hours every week and see for yourself how authentic, effective cold calling can really boost your numbers.

Set Your Intention Before Calling

As you may have noticed I'm big on intentions. Everything in the universe begins with intentions. When you decide to stand up, sit down, buy a cheeseburger or make a cold call, it all starts with an intention.

After I have prepared myself mentally, emotionally, physically and spiritually I consciously set my cold calling intentions. My first intention is to call prospects and set an appointment as I KNOW I have a product and/or service that is beneficial to my potential customer. My intention is to be of service and value to the prospect, having only their best interests at heart. I intend on hearing YES from prospects.

I have no intention of discussing existing service or billing issues or solving problems on this call. All existing customer issues or problems can and will be addressed at our meeting, I kindly and sympathetically state. Actually, issues are a blessing in disguise as there is now urgency involved and a meeting can be set for the next day.

I intend to be brief, concise, to the point, and off the phone within a few minutes with an appointment set. Another intention I go in with is setting the day, date and time of the appointment. For every call I make I have mentally designated the day, date and time I want to meet with the prospect. If the prospect is agreeable to meeting with me I ask them, "Does 10 a.m. on Wednesday the 15th work for you?". If the morning is not convenient for them I always have my second choice in mind which is usually the same day and in the afternoon.

Very seldom does the prospect say it has to be in a week or more out and I only agree to this if I feel they are not just blowing me off and the reason sounds legitimate. You will be able to tell if they are truthful or not by the degree of sincerity they express.

As a rule I only set appointments a day or two out because, given time to think about it, the prospect can come up with a litany of reasons why they can't meet. For this same reason I never call to confirm the appointment as experience has taught me the prospect will begin the conversation with, "I'm glad you called..." as they gently deflate you with a cancellation.

In summary, set your intentions to setting an appointment by being brief, to the point and concise, not discussing issues or problems on the call and knowing in advance the day, date and time you are setting the appointment for. It has always works for me and it will work for you.

Don't Argue, Don't Defend, Always Play Nice

Let's face some brutal realities. Occasionally, you will encounter harsh, angry, critical prospects that have had a bad experience with your company or they simply don't understand how regulated utilities work and will release their venom upon you.

Don't take it personally when you get dumped on, as everybody has a bad day and misery loves company. I can honestly say that it does not happen often as most people maintain some sense of decorum even when present life is a struggle for them. No matter what a prospect throws at you always, always, remain cool and calm. Be courteous and polite, project confidence and at the end of your discussion honestly thank them for their time whether you set an appointment or not.

When a prospect starts to complain about my company's services, products, billing procedures, service issues, etc., I simply agree with them. I refuse to defend my position against any complaint because you know as well as I do that every telecommunications company, any company for that matter, has experienced customer problems in all areas of operations. You will be amazed at how quickly the complaining prospect's argument deflates when you agree that you suck.

"Your right Bob, I've been doing this a long time and you're not the first customer this has happened to. We are dealing with a large company and sometimes these things happen. I am very sorry it happened to you." After I say something like this the prospect usually pauses, as I know I've baffled them, and moves right on to the next topic. I have listened to them, acknowledged their pain and apologized. The issue is closed and they feel they have been heard so why beat a dead horse. Try it, you'll be astonished at how easy it is to temper a potentially volatile situation.

When you are polite and respectful to everyone you talk to you are validating the importance of their time. I have had prospects ignite at the mention of my companies name but after diffusing them I sometimes get the appointment. I cold call offering value and a possible solution to an existing problem so after the rant, a calmer and cost conscious mind usually surfaces and we move forward. Even if the prospect doesn't get it yet, I know my product or service is going to be of benefit to them so I stay strong and ride the wave out.

Call Your Warm Leads First

I always call my warm leads first when I begin a cold calling session. As you recall a warm lead is an existing customer that currently utilizes one or more of your products or services. You have the contact name and you know their current level of service, and the products they use because you accessed your company's customer database and obtained this information.

Starting with warm leads quickly builds your confidence, as a current customer is more apt to take your call and most quite receptive to what you have to offer often quite receptive to what you have to offer. It's so much easier to get past gatekeepers as most of them recognize their company is already a customer of yours and won't question the nature of your call.

Not only do warm leads increase the conversion rate of your funnel they provide you the opportunity to meet with a customer who has never met with a rep from your company before. You can become a trusted source of contact, advise, and help for them whether they buy now or not. You never know how far your unconditional support will ripple out.

A bit more on calling warm leads as a confidence builder. Starting your cold calling session by calling warm leads decreases fear, anxiety, and apprehension related to cold calling prospects. It's much easier calling existing customers and this will get you into the flow of calling prospects and you may set your appointment quota before you know it. After you have gained your confidence mix up your calls between warm leads and cold leads. As you become more confident in this practice, cold calling may actually become enjoyable and fulfilling for you.

Contacting Decision Makers

It doesn't matter how great a product or service you are offering, if you can't get to the decision maker you're wasting your time and diminishing the possibility of setting an appointment. Your intention is to meet with the decision maker and, after discovering their needs: and providing your products and services meet their needs, get a quote into their hands.

You should have a contact name for most of your leads so now you want to start building a relationship with the prospect. In my experience I find the secretary asks what company I'm with about 50% of the time. Very nice when they don't ask as you don't have to deal with the gatekeeper and can proceed without impedance.

If you are put through without any interference and the decision maker doesn't answer and you get voicemail DO NOT leave a message. <u>All the cold calling books I have read have a section on leaving voicemails that are effective and I can tell you that is nonsense.</u> Usually, they will not call you back and more likely than not will tell the front desk to block you when you call again. It's tempting to leave a message and a great deterrent to actually talking with the decision maker but it just plain doesn't work and most likely and you will have blown any chance of getting an appointment. Make a note in your "Notes" section to call back later.

It is important to realize you will call some prospects many times over several months before you ever reach them. It's just part of the process so don't be discouraged. I have called prospects for almost a year before I finally made contact with them. More often than not I got the appointment primarily because this type of individual is extremely busy and quick to listen to opportunities and quick to decide yea or nay on your proposal. So don't give up!

Turn Gatekeepers Into Allies

I have used the term "gatekeeper" in preceding sections and now is the time to address this sometimes overly protective executive assistant or receptionist, with whom you may often engage. Do not fall into the trap of thinking of them as opponents or as someone you can outsmart and/or outmaneuver. Instead develop the mindset that this individual can be a vital ally, filled to the brim with insider information who may have their finger on the pulse of the company and; quite probably yields some influence.

Gatekeepers are quite often overworked, underpaid and not appreciated. I always go out of my way to be kind and considerate to gatekeepers and, when asked, am always very forthcoming with information about who I am and why I am calling. As I said, sometimes you have to call and call before establishing contact with the decision maker so don't alienate the person guarding the door. Many times I have called a company back; the gatekeeper remembered me and we end up having quite a friendly little chat. In short, don't bite the hand that may feed you.

If you don't have a contact name ask the gatekeeper for their help. Human nature instinctively responds to a plea for help. I tell them my name, my company and why I am calling. I ask them for their help in identifying the individual that makes the decisions for the product or service I am offering. I say, "Alice, maybe you can help me, I'm looking for the person that makes the decision for your communications. Can you tell me who that is?" Be conversational and friendly but not unctuous! I almost always get a name and immediately write it down. I also write down the name of the gatekeeper and use it during our conversation and use it to greet them if I have to call back. Occasionally they won't give you the decision makers name and ask for your name and number instead. Just give it to them and thank them for their time and for passing along your information. We'll cover ways to get around this situation shortly.

If the gatekeeper gives you the decision makers name and tells you the person is not in or unavailable, do not let them send you to voicemail. Ask if there is a better time to call, or if there is an alternative way to contact the decision maker. Asking for their advice shows respect for their knowledge and validates their importance to you as a source of valuable information.

Every once in a while you will encounter the gatekeeper who wants to know who you are, why you are calling, your shoe size, and what you had for breakfast. After you cheerfully volunteer the information and ask for their help with contacting the decision maker, they will promptly tell you the company is not interested. Don't be frazzled, press on with this question, "Do you make that decision?" 99.9% percent of the time the answer is a disgruntled, "NO!" You have now challenged their imaginary position of authority and pissed them off so you have nothing to lose by pushing forward. Ask them who then makes that decision. They will either give you a name, not give you a name, or say that person is not available and ask for your phone number to pass on if the decision maker is interested. If you get a name you will have to ask to be put through as this person is still smoldering. Usually they ask for your number so give them the number and move on.

When you have a gatekeeper like the one I just described or if you had a pleasant gatekeeper but still had to leave your number there are two things you can do. One is to call before 8 a.m. or after 5 p.m. as the gatekeeper will be gone and someone else will answer the phone. Either the decision maker answers the call or someone who's job description doesn't include screening calls will answer and put you right through. The second option is to find another direct line into the business or if auto attend answers choose any extension and request the information you need from whoever answers. Both alternatives work the majority of the time.

So now you know how this process works and blends together so I want to share with you what I say when I cold call prospects. I cold call with the intent to set appointments for three categories of the sales paradigm. These three categories are:

1. "warm leads" which are current customers utilizing at least one product or service I sell.
2. "new business" which are businesses that have never been a customer of my company.
3. "win-backs" are previous customers that have switched to another carrier.

It's All How You Say It

You have your quality prospect list, prepared yourself mentally, emotionally, physically and spiritually and know how to deal with gatekeepers but don't have a clue what you are going to say to the prospect. Not a problem! Always keep in mind that my style of cold calling is unscripted yet does have structure.

When I call a prospect my intention is to secure an appointment and spend no more than three to four minutes to do so. I don't engage in small talk and when I reach the decision maker I introduce myself, identify my company, pitch my value statement, set the appointment, schedule another time if they request it, or mark them off as not interested at this time. If they are under contract I make a note to put a tickler in my CRM system, enter the contract expiration date and any other pertinent observations.

The following are examples of what I say to prospects when I cold call and responses you can expect from the other end of the line. After years of cold calling I believe I can accurately supply you with the most typical prospect reactions and replies. Keep in mind that you are not going by a script and that you will have to adapt to however the conversation goes. This can only come by experience but to gain that experience you have to start somewhere.

I always start with warm leads, because as I stated earlier, they are more receptive to my call and can quickly build your confidence. Here is a sample of my warm lead cold calling pitch. Please note that I always address the prospect by their first name. I don't care who they are I call them by their first name as this establishes immediate rapport and puts me on a equal level with them.

The Warm Lead Pitch

WARM LEAD COLD CALL

Me: Hi Mary, my name is (your name) and I'm with (your company). You currently have us for your internet service but I noticed you have your business lines with someone else. I'm curious, has anyone from (your company name) come to your office, personally met with you and given you a quote for bundled service? The reason I ask is that we can usually save our customers a fair amount of money by bundling services and I just want to get a quote in your hands to see if I can help you.

Prospect: No they haven't.

Me: Are you available tomorrow at 10 a.m.?

Prospect: (After checking schedule) 10 a.m. is fine.

Me: Good, I'll see you tomorrow morning at 10. Thanks for your time and I'll see you soon.

Sound too easy? Well it really is this simple. Too much ado is made out of cold calling and I have seen more books and websites that want you to believe it's a scientific, complicated process that needs to follow an established script. I have found that to be untrue! My way is not the only way, nor do I claim it to be the perfect way but it has been effective and simple to use.

More on warm calling: After your intro, value statement and question about a previous meeting with a

rep from your company the ideal answer is the one in my example. Believe it or not I have set a huge amount of appointments with this simple pitch and it happened just the way I shared with you. Other answers you will hear are:
1. "I have never met with someone but now is not a good time." Great, just means there is a better time so ask when that is and set a date to call them back.
2. "Yes we did meet with someone and the savings weren't enough to warrant a change." Unless you have new cost saving promos to offer them, thank them for their time and state you will call back when promos come up if that's OK with them. If you do have a hot promo at the time tell them about it and ask for the appointment to revisit the quote.
3. "No, and we are not interested." Stop right there. My initial thought was that this was a challenge, which I needed to meet. Experience has taught me that trying to convince them otherwise is usually an exercise in futility. Why waste their time or yours when you could be calling someone who might be more receptive. Kindly thank them for their time, mark them off your list and move forward to the next call.
4. Many times the prospect will tell you what they like and dislike about your service or product. Acknowledge their statement and confirm you will cover issues, positive or negative, when you meet with them.

You are not reading from a script so you will have to learn to go with the flow of the conversation. Conversations will vary and other responses will occur. Always stay calm, don't chase the sale or the prospect. Think before you speak and never be adversarial or minimize the prospects concerns. The point is you are not making a sales call buy rather creating value and establishing trust as an advisor. Stick to your intentions and allow the outcome to develop as it will.

I love warm leads as my conversion rate of warm lead calls to appointments is very high. I haven't taken time to calculate a true percentage rate but off the top of my head I can calculate the success rate to be slightly better than 40%. In the realm of cold calling that, my friends, is a substantial rate of success. Cold calling can also yield a high rate of conversion from call to established appointment, as the pitch is basically the same. The only difference, of course, being that the warm call is an established customer whereas the cold call is a new prospect. That said; let's explore the art of cold calling for new business.

The New Business Pitch

While nurturing your existing customer's level of satisfaction is important, obtaining new business is vital. Generating new business is essential if you want to make it in the telecommunications industry. The good news here is that every business that utilizes telecommunications, and is not presently with your company, is a new business prospect.

Cold calling prospects for new business isn't all that different from the warm lead pitch you just learned about. I have noticed the majority of business owners and IT departments are not adverse to changing carriers for lower costs if they can secure comparable or improved services and features.

It gets a bit complicated here as you may encounter previous customers when cold calling for new business. This situation falls into the win-back category, which can be tricky, but are also an opportunity if handled correctly. We shall explore the correct strategy for win-backs after we finish how to obtain new business.

Here's what I say to potential new customers:

Me: Hi Mary, my name is (your name) and I'm with (your company). I noticed you are currently with another carrier and I'm curious, has anyone from (your company name) come to your office, personally met with you and given you a quote for our service? The reason I ask is that we can save business owners (or companies depending on who you're dealing with; owner, IT, CFO) a fair amount of money by bundling services and I just want to get a quote in your hands to see if I can help you.

Prospect: No they haven't.

Me: Are you available tomorrow at 10 a.m.?

Prospect: (After checking schedule) 10 a.m. is fine.

Me: Good, I'll see you tomorrow morning at 10. Thanks for your time and I'll see you soon.

Once again this is an ideal scenario and it does, sometimes, happen. Actually, more often than I ever thought it would so using this as a basic pitch will get the ball rolling with the prospect. Of course, you will encounter many other responses after the opening and I will list as many as I can recall experiencing over the years. Really most of the replies you will receive are the same ones from your warm lead calls so forgive me if I am redundant but it's worth the time and space to repeat them.

1. "I'm not interested." No problems, kindly thank them for their time, mark them off the list and move on.
2. "We are under contract." So get contract expiration date, note the date, and tell them you will be in touch a month before their contract expires.
3. "I have never met with someone but now is not a good time." Cool, just means there is a better time so ask when that is and set a date to call them back.
4. "Yes we did meet with someone and the savings weren't enough to warrant a change." Unless you have new cost saving promos to offer them, thank them for their time and state you will call back when promos come up if that's OK with them. If you do have a hot promo at the time tell them about it and ask for the appointment to revisit the quote.
5. "You are the worst company I have ever dealt with...You suck, etc." Tell them you're sorry they've had such a terrible experience, graciously thank them for their time and mark them off.
6. "Can you email me the quote?" In a word, NO! The reason is you don't have a clue as to what their existing service consists of and the only way to find out is to meet face to face. Explain this to them. It's astoundingly logical when you think about it.
7. "I don't make that decision." No problem. Ask for the name of the decision maker, if you can be transferred to them or when is the best time to call back.
8. "My IT department (or someone else) takes care of that." This is perfect if you are speaking to the to the owner, CEO, CFO or executive officer! Get that contact person's name and extension or direct telephone number, ask if you can be transferred and when you talk to them, or even if you have to call them back, tell them you just spoke to (give the name of the person that referred you to them) and that he or she wanted you to make an appointment with them so you can deliver a quote. Nothing better than top-down selling!
9. "Give me your number and I'll call you back." Chances are they never will call you back. This is an excuse to get you off the phone and the prospect doesn't have the internal fortitude to blow you off. Leave your number, make a note that you did with date, and call them back in a month or two. Persistence pays off.

As my cold calling system is unscripted and free flowing you always have to able to improvise. You don't have to be pushy, desperate or defensive. Actually a casual attitude is more effective as the prospect can and will detect your subtle, confident manner and respond in similar fashion. Always keep in mind that there are many other prospects that will meet with you and buy from you so never take a prospect's rejection personally. Your self-worth and true value is not based on their good opinion, and quite frankly their opinion is none of your business.

I have had many prospects tell me my timing couldn't be better because their current service is always being interrupted and/or they have spent hours of wasted time dealing with billing issues that are never resolved. They are primed to move carriers and will jump at your most favorable offer.

This is not always the case and you will have to call previous customers that left due to price, and service or billing issues. So how do you win them back? Truthfully it can be a challenge but prospects addressed with compassion and product knowledge can be won back, so now let's look at the opportunities presented in the win-back category.

The Win-Back Pitch

Customers leave a carrier for three main reasons. The first being price, the second being consistent service issues, and the third being constant billing conflicts. The growing cost of telecommunications is becoming a major consideration for companies when choosing a carrier. I would say most customers leave their provider based solely on cost. They understand how the business works today. They know they can lock in a fair price now, which will be good for three years, at which time they will negotiate for a better or same rate, or jump ship to another provider and repeat the process again in three years.

Before you attempt to call win-backs educate yourself on your companies win-back policies and promos as well as FCC regulations about your products and service and state regulations as imposed by your Utility Regulatory Commission. You have to know what tariffs are and how they affect your customer and the way you do business. I suggest you research all the information available from your company resources, your local Utility Regulatory Commission website, the FCC website and the Utilities and Transportation Commission website.

Let me give you an example of how important this information can be when calling win-back prospects. I cold called win-back prospects located in Indiana for almost two years straight. After my intro and basic pitch, the vast majority of prospects would say, "Well why didn't you give me a better price when I was with you?" At this juncture my homework about tariffs and utility commissions was my saving grace and the doorway to an appointment. I was calling for a national carrier who was, and still is, highly regulated by the FCC and the Indiana Utility Regulatory Commission which means as far as pricing goes their hands are tied.

I would say to the prospect, "We couldn't give you a better price then because we're a regulated utility, just like the gas, water and electric company. You don't even think about calling those utilities to try and negotiate a better price because you know it can't be done. Our pricing is determined by the Indiana Utility Regulatory Commission, which *does allow* for special pricing when it comes to earning your business back. I am asking you for the opportunity to earn your business back."

This approach usually left the prospect speechless because they didn't have a clue as to how the telecom industry works. All they know is that a CLEC or a provider exempted from telecommunications service regulations called or a national carrier with win-back promo pricing called and offered the same service for a better price and the rest is history. It is essential that you be heavily armed with information, and that you can explain in an understandable manner to succeed at win-backs. It was a bit of a struggle at first but I persevered and after a short time was booking win-back appointments on a regular basis that resulted in a fair amount of the business.

The basic approach is the same as warm lead and new business calling with the difference being what happens after the initial pitch.

WIN-BACK COLD CALL (IDEAL BUT RARE)

Me: Hi Mary, my name is (your name) and I'm with (your company). I know you were once with us and the reason I called is that I would like to make an appointment with you to see if I can earn your business back. We can save business owners (or companies depending on who you're dealing with; owner, IT, CFO) that return to us a fair amount of money by bundling services and I just want to get a quote in your hands to see if I can help you.

Prospect: No they haven't.

Me: Are you available tomorrow at 10 a.m.?

Prospect: (After checking schedule) 10 a.m. is fine.

Me: Good, I'll see you tomorrow morning at 10. Thanks for your time and I'll see you soon.

MOST LIKELY SCENARIO

Me: Hi Mary, my name is (your name) and I'm with (your company name). I know you were once with us and the reason I called is that I would like to make an appointment with you to see if I can earn your business back. We can save business owners (or companies depending on who you're dealing with; owner, IT, CFO) that return to us, a fair amount of money by bundling services and I just want to get a quote in your hands to see if I can help you.

Prospect: Why didn't you give me better pricing when I was with you?

Me: "We couldn't give you a better price then because we're a regulated utility, just like the gas, water and electric company. You don't even think about calling those utilities to try and negotiate a better price because you know it can't be done. Our pricing is determined by the Indiana Utility Regulatory Commission which does allow for special pricing when it comes to earning your business back. I am asking you for the opportunity to earn your business back."

As you can see anything can happen at this point. This is why a free flow style works where a script fails. A script doesn't allow for confrontation, which can lead to the cold caller becoming frustrated and panicky. Become fluid in your approach. Find out more about why the customer left and what you can do to regain their business. Unless they immediately tell you your company blows and they will never do business with you again, let your sales personality and natural caring abilities come out. Honestly strive to be of service to this prospect. When your potential customer sees that you genuinely care about them rather than just trying to make a sale, you will be surprised at the results.

I strongly suggest you make lots and lots of warm and new biz calls before attempting win-backs. Reason is, you will have gained invaluable cold calling communication skills and will have fielded most types of objections and have dealt with many different personalities.

When calling win-backs you have to learn to roll with the punches, as you never know what you are venturing into. You will encounter very unhappy former customers that have been silently lingering in the depths of telecommunications despair, just waiting for the opportunity to cut the head off any rep from your company that has the audacity to call them.

Years of frustration, concealed anger and burning resentment will flow forth from the mouths of people that are normally mentally and emotionally balanced. You just happened to have opened the gates of hell for them and are going to be the object of their pent up anger and frustration. Let them proceed. Don't interrupt, don't defend, don't bend over, just let the venom stream until they are done. Tell them you understand, you are sorry they had such a horrific experience and thank them for their time. Much of the time, just the exercise of venting their pent up anger will go a long way to resolving the situation. This is your opportunity to empathize with them by letting them know you understand their concerns and would like to be given the opportunity to give them the service they deserve. You may or may not get the opportunity to present them with a quote, but they will invariably feel better about your company than they used to, which may lead to an opportunity in the future. You have planted a seed, which you or someone else may see mature into future business.

You may recognize this line from the soliloquy in the "Nunnery Scene" of the play *Hamlet* by William Shakespeare, " To be, or not to be: that is the question: Whether 'tis nobler in the mind to suffer The slings and arrows of outrageous fortune, Or to take arms against a sea of troubles, And by opposing end them?" When it comes to win-backs you must suffer the slings and arrows of past bad experiences to become immune to them and move forward. If you do so and carry on I promise you there will often be gold at the end of the rainbow.

Don't Stop Once You Start

Once you have begun your cold calling session do not stop for any reason. Go to the bathroom before you begin and complete all scheduled calls or tasks before you ever pick up the phone. It's fine to pause and jot down remarks in the "Notes" section of your list, or to enter info into your CRM system but move on to the next call quickly.

You will encounter challenging personalities so be prepared to accept whatever comes your way and set the intention that such individuals will not affect your next call. I play golf and have played since I was twelve years old. I had to learn early on that when I had a bad shot I had to put it out of my mind before my next shot or I was doomed to repeat the same mistake. It's a game of ebb and flow and so is cold calling.

You will discover a natural rhythm comes over you as you are making calls. A sense of accomplishment prevails and your positive energy builds with each call. Any prolonged break or waiting period allows your focus and energy to slip away and it's difficult to get back into the game after that happens.

Use Your Intuition

Rarely did I just go down my list calling prospects in the order they appeared. I selected who I would call by using my intuition, or instinct if you will. Intuition is having a innate inclination toward a certain action or behavior without any analytic reasoning. Don't be discouraged if you feel you lack this at the outset. The more you do this the more naturally it will come

I would scan my list, not thinking specifically about any certain prospect until a name leaped out at me. Call it a gut feeling or a hunch but when I noticed this sensation and acted on it I was usually successful in setting the appointment.

We all have this inner "guidance system" it's just that we haven't developed it, don't believe in it, or simply refuse to listen to it. Winston Churchill once exclaimed, "...in truth, all people are offered help by their intuition - but most pick themselves up and escape as fast as possible."

Begin to let your instincts guide you. As you do you will become better and better at knowing who to call and when to call them. It's actually a form of unconscious reasoning, which will stand you in good stead not just in sales but also in all facets of life.

CONCLUSION

When I was in college I took script writing and instructional writing classes and being a communications major, the required speech classes. In the instructional writing and speech classes I soon learned Aristotle's "triptych" which in essence is; Tell them what you are going to tell them, tell them, then tell them what you just told them.

In the introduction I told you cold calling is still a viable and essential part of your selling strategy yet is overlooked by so many because of the fear factor involved and lack of knowledge of the "how to" of cold calling. I also told you this was written with the telecommunications professional in mind and the system and methods I have written about actually apply to anyone in the sales arena. I stated my system is not a scripted style of cold calling but more of a free flowing, personality adapting, evolutionary method that will help you get past the fear of cold calling and will generate more business than you are currently experiencing.

I spoke to you of the two basic motivating forces, how to build quality lists, how to prepare mentally, emotionally, physically and spiritually, and last but not least, the art of cold calling. Now I am telling you what I have expressed to you will diminish your cold calling resistance, will help you continually meet or exceed your monthly quota, and may assist you with preparations for activities inside and outside of work.

Cold calling is most effective when used with the intention to serve the growth and development of the client and the salesperson. High pressure or desperate selling is not selling at all; it's self serving manipulation. It may generate some business but as with any coerced activity it will eventually weaken and collapse. Strive to be authentic, seeking solutions that empower your customer or prospect and you will witness spectacular results.

I hope you found this information enlightening and beneficial and perhaps I made you smile from time to time. Again, my prayer for all of you is unlimited prosperity and success in all you choose to undertake and accomplish in this life.

Namaste - I bow to the divine in you.

I openly welcome any and all thoughts, positive or not feedback, praises or critiques. Please email me at: enlightenedcoldcalling@gmail.com

www.ingramcontent.com/pod-product-compliance
Lightning Source LLC
Chambersburg PA
CBHW070907220526
45466CB00005B/2152